I was once approached by a friend who surprisingly commented, "I wish I had one of *YOUR* Bibles." I was stunned upon hearing this statement. With a puzzled demeanor I asked my friend, "why do you want *MY* Bible." She explained that her experience reading the bible was always one of confusion and disorientation. My friend believed that reading the Bible alongside my notes and perspective would help her gain a new, fresh understanding of the Bible.

Following this conversation, I thoroughly contemplated the idea of actually giving one of my Bibles, filled with all my notes and highlights, to one person at the end of the year. I had over 500 people express interest in the first few hours after mentioning this proposition on social media. Upon the flood of interest, my friend encouraged me to start typing my notes and share them within a topic-specific Facebook group. Through the Facebook group, I had several people ask me about putting that same content in a tangible book so that they could follow along and take notes of their own.

Today, you hold that journey in your hands. To be honest, I never thought I would be the person to write anything of this nature. However, in hindsight, I can see that God has always had this detail as part of His plan. My prayer is that you fall in love with your Bible like never before. I pray that this study will help you understand God's Word, and that you will see Jesus throughout every page as you study alongside me.

Thanks for joining the journey!

XOXO

GENESIS

Author: Moses

Genesis is a foundational book for theology. In it, we understand who God is and the original plan for man. Throughout this book, people fail but God continues to reach out to them. Most of Genesis focuses on Abraham, Isaac, and Jacob. Abraham is known as the Father of Faith (Romans 3:27–4:25), which is why the New Testament often points back to him and his faith.

TABLE OF CONTENTS

Genesis 1 7

Genesis 2 9

Genesis 3 11

Genesis 4 14

Genesis 5 19

Genesis 6 20

Genesis 7 22

Genesis 8 23

Genesis 9 25

Genesis 10 26

Genesis 11 27

Genesis 12 30

Genesis 13 34

Genesis 14 38

Genesis 15 40

Genesis 16 42

Genesis 17 44

Genesis 18 46

Genesis 19 48

Genesis 20 50

Genesis 21 52

Genesis 22 56

Genesis 23 60

Genesis 24 62

Genesis 25 66

Genesis 26 69

Genesis 27 74

Genesis 28 76

Genesis 29 78

Genesis 30 79

Genesis 31 80

Genesis 32 84

Genesis 33 86

Genesis 34 89

Genesis 35 93

Genesis 36 97

Genesis 37 100

Genesis 38 105

Genesis 39 107

Genesis 40 110

Genesis 41 111

Genesis 42 115

Genesis 43 119

Genesis 44 121

Genesis 45 123

Genesis 46 125

Genesis 47 126

Genesis 48 128

Genesis 49 129

Genesis 50 134

About Crystal Sparks 136

GENESIS 1

Contrast this chapter with John 1. The book of John is often called the Genesis for New Testament believers. In John, God finished perfectly what He began in Genesis.

Read John 1:1–5. Contrast it with Genesis 1:1–5. What similarities do you see?

Genesis 1:11

I love how *The Amplified* says, "whose seed is in them."

This tells us two things:

1. When God created us, He put everything we need on the inside of us. We lack nothing. So when God formed you, He made you with the right amount of gifts, talents, and abilities. There is no need to worry or stress that you are lacking anything.

2. God made you with multiplication in mind. What God starts in you, won't stop with you. God works in you so others can be impacted through you.

Genesis 1:26

Underline the words "complete authority" in your Bible. God made us to rule and reign. From the very beginning, He gave us all power to conquer. He never intended you to be a victim to this life or to circumstances.

Genesis 1:31

GOD APPROVED OF YOU BEFORE ANYONE COULD REJECT YOU.

He gave mankind the assignment to rule and reign before they did anything to disobey Him. Yet, He knew that Adam and Eve would sin He was already pleased with them. Just as He is with you. When you wake each morning, God is pleased with you!

GENESIS 2

Genesis 2:2

God did not *need* to rest. He made the choice to rest. Rest is not a sign of weakness but strength. We are made in God's image, so we are designed for rest.

Genesis 2:11–12

Recently, when I read these verses again, they blew my mind in a whole new way. What does it say was in the land? Think about this: God gave them gold. Even before there was a currency system, He knew they would need it eventually, so He gave them provision for *future needs*!

If money is evil, then why would God give it to them in the first two chapters of creation?

Genesis 2:15

The Amplified Bible says they were to "cultivate and keep" what God had given them. Everything God gives us is our responsibility to cultivate and keep.

- Our children
- Homes
- Finances
- Businesses

Genesis 2:19

GOD LOVES FOR US TO BE A PART OF WHAT HE IS DOING.

He could have named all the animals Himself, but instead He involved man. Adam named *every* animal. Not only that, Adam was able to remember what he named them! God made our minds to be strong and our memory to be perfect.

GENESIS 3

Genesis 3:1

Listening to the enemy always causes you to question God's Word. (See Matthew 4:1–11.) God's Word is God's will. So when the enemy can get you to question the Word of God, he also causes you to question God's will (purpose) for your life.

Jesus is referred to as the second Adam. How was Jesus' response to the enemy different from Adam's in Matthew 4?

How has the enemy caused you to question God's Word/will for your life?

How do you respond when the devil brings into question God's Word?

Genesis 3:10

Shame drives us into hiding. When we owe someone money, we avoid them. When we mess up, we miss church. When we lie about something, we avoid the topic. Shame leads us away from healing into hiding.

Genesis 3:11–13

God asked, "Who told you that?" He knew the answer but asked anyway. For us to remove the power of lies we believe, we must discover the source of when and where the belief took hold.

Instead of acknowledging the wrong belief, Adam blamed someone else. God did not offer a solution until His question was answered and the source was identified. So often, the lies we believe still control us because we are unwilling to understand when and where they started.

For example, we live in lack because we were told all our lives money was evil.

WE DON'T ATTEMPT BIG THINGS BECAUSE WE WERE TOLD WE COULD NEVER BE SUCCESSFUL.

Genesis 3:17
There were two parts to Adam's disobedience. He listened and heeded.
Behavior is always the result of our thinking, and our thinking is molded by the voice we listen to most. Adam and Eve had no problems with sin when they were only listening to God.

What you listen to, you will act on.

Genesis 3:21
Blood was shed for the first time. God sacrificed animals for the remission of their sins and to cover their shame. (See Hebrews 9:14,22.) For the first time, sin entered the earth and God's salvation plan began. For the rest of the Old Testament, the blood of animals was shed for people to receive forgiveness. Jesus came to satisfy the wrath of God. (See Hebrews 10:1–8.)

Genesis 3:22
If they had eaten from the tree of life (even though they sinned), they would have lived forever in their fallen state. God loved them too much to let that happen, so He removed them from the garden.

Genesis 4

Genesis 4:1
Eve gave birth to the first child. I often wonder what her experience was like. She had no sisters, mother, or medical professionals to encourage and guide her. I cannot imagine Adam's shock as she gave birth.

Genesis 4:3–4
There are a few things I want to point out to you that we will study together in a moment. I think doing this together will help you understand it better and will help you to be able to go back in your Bible later and remember what we studied.

One of my favorite things about reading my Bible is seeing my notes and highlights from when I have read it before. I would love for you to leave some marks in your Bible as we read this together! Underline the phrases "in the course of time" and "firstborn of his flock."

Genesis 4:4–6
Why did God have respect for one offering and not the other? What was the difference?

Read Proverbs 3:9, Deuteronomy 26:1–2, and Exodus 23:19.

God is a God of the first. Scripture doesn't say God was upset at Cain, but rather he preferred Abel's offering. If you want God's favor, give Him the first in all you have and do. (See Matthew 6:33.)

Write thoughts about the above mentioned scriptures:

Are you giving God your first?

Genesis 4:8–9

Anger is murder in seed form. (See Matthew 5:21–22.) Cain was jealous of the favor given to Abel and wanted it for himself.

Later, there would be another, Judas, who would act the same way. His actions would also end in murder. (See John 12:1–6 and Matthew 26:14–16.)

Where have you been critical of the favor on other people's lives?

Are you honoring God with the first or are you giving Him your leftovers?

Genesis 4:10
God heard blood speak.

Genesis 4:15
God protected Cain even though he was in sin.

Genesis 4:16–24
Cain's fierce anger at the rejection of his offering shows his self-righteousness. The murder of his brother was an act of defiance against the God who showed favor to his brother. Instead of changing something about himself, Cain removed the person that was his competition. As a

result, he left the presence of the Lord and went to Nod (which means wandering).

It seems like Cain got away with his act of disobedience. In verses 17–22, things are going well for Cain. However, his consequences will catch up to him later through his descendants. In verses 23–24, the scene goes bleak.

Lamech's act of anger was answered by the goodness of God's grace.

Contrast Genesis 4:24 with Matthew 18:21–22.

Genesis 4:25–26

Again, God restored to Eve what seemed to be lost. Eve's faith declared, "God has appointed for me another child." The literally translation is "another seed." She was referring to Genesis 3:15 when God said her seed would crush the head of the enemy.

I love how the commentary *Genesis: beginning and blessing* explains the birth of Seth:

"Cain's firstborn and successors pioneer cities and civilized arts, but Seth's firstborn and successors pioneer worship."[1]

---

[1] Hughes, R. K. (2004). *Genesis: beginning and blessing* (p. 115). Wheaton, IL: Crossway Books.

After a chapter full of heartbreak and loss, the end is beautiful. God's plans always prevail. Even when men's choices seem to deviate, God still finds a way. Read Romans 8:28.

How does this chapter give you confidence that God is working on your behalf?

GENESIS 5

Genesis 5:1

Compare and contrast with Genesis 5:3. What similarities do you see?

Who do you look like?

Genesis 5:32

Note Noah's age when he had his sons. I want you to see his age to know that even when the world considers us old, God views us as just getting started. You are never too old (or too young for that matter) to start a new season in God!

GENESIS 6

Genesis 6:5
Note what was evil. It doesn't say their deeds; it talks about their thoughts. God desires our minds to be renewed (Romans 12:2).

Genesis 6:8–9
What did Noah find?

Why do you think he did?

How was Noah's description similar to Enoch's in Genesis 5:24?

Genesis 6:11

The earth reflected the state of their thinking.

What about your life? Does your thinking change the world around you?

Genesis 6:14–16

God gave Noah an assignment with specific instructions. In our lives, God will ask us to do something *then* tell us how to accomplish it.

Genesis 6:17

This was the first rain. Noah had no point of reference for what God was talking about.

Genesis 6:22

God picked Noah because He knew Noah would be faithful to do what He commanded.

God chose you because He knew you would be faithful to all He tells you to do.

GENESIS 7

Genesis 7:1
How much of his household was Noah to bring?
God desires our entire household to be saved. (See
Joshua 6:25 and Acts 16:25–40.)

Genesis 7:4
Forty is the number of trial or testing.[2]

Genesis 7:6
Note Noah's age now. How many years have gone by
since Genesis 5:32?

Genesis 7:4 and 7:24
Can you imagine 40 days of rain and 150 days with
water? That's nearly 200 days on a boat with your
family and all the animals of the earth. I am sure
Noah felt like, "This is more than I signed up for!"

What situation are you facing that makes you feel like
Noah?

---

[2] Thompson, Adam F., Beale, Adrian. *The Divinity Code to Understanding
Your Dreams and Visions*. Destiny Image: December 2011.

Genesis 8:1

Not only did God remember Noah, but He *earnestly* remembered him.[3] (See Isaiah 49:16.)

GOD NEVER LEADS YOU THEN LEAVES YOU. HE DIDN'T BRING YOU THIS FAR TO FAIL YOU!

Genesis 8:7–8

First, Noah sent out a raven, symbolizing the works of the flesh. The dove represented the Holy Spirit.

The raven never returned. Works done in our flesh never produce anything. Works done by the Spirit of God always bring peace.

Genesis 8:20–21

The first action Noah took was to sacrifice to the Lord. (Remember Cain and Abel.) What was God's response to Noah's sacrifice and obedience?

---

[3] *AMPC*

Take a moment and recognize how pleased God is with you as you spend time in His Word and are faithful in giving.

GENESIS 9

Genesis 9:1
He is the God of "but wait there is more." God blessed them and made covenant with them in the last chapter, then continued to promise even more.

Genesis 9:1–17
Along with the blessing, God gave directions to Noah, repeating much of what He told Adam initially. Some have said our command to reign in the earth stopped with Adam because of his sin. These verses prove the opposite.

Genesis 9:20–21
Noah came out of a powerful moment and got drunk. Sometimes our highest moments with God are followed by our lowest moments of humanity.

Genesis 9:25
Ham's consequence came upon his son. What we do in our lifetime sometimes isn't fully realized until the next generation.

GENESIS 10

In chapter 9, Noah spoke of what was to come in his family. Then in chapter 10, his words play out over the next generations. I love when genealogies are listed in scripture. They show the faithfulness of God throughout generations.

Think about your family tree? How is your relationship with God shaping your family for the better?

After Noah's drunken debacle, each of his sons separated themselves from the family and began their own nations.

GENESIS 11

Genesis 11:1
The people were all of one language.

Genesis 11:5
God notices what we are building.

Genesis 11:6–7
Compare this verse to Ephesians 3:20. What major difference do you see?

God didn't say what they were doing was impossible. Building a tower to Heaven was possible as long as they were unified and speaking the same language. Verse 7 shows how God stopped their progress.

Read Ephesians 4:3, Acts 2:1–4.

If I was the enemy, how would I stop God's people from building something great? I would keep them divided against each other and not speaking the same language.

The baptism of the Holy Spirit is God restoring what was lost in Genesis! That is why the enemy fights against people in believing in the power of praying in the spirit. He knows when we are all speaking the same language (our prayer language) then there is nothing we can't do!

Genesis 11:26–31

Abraham's father, Terah, had three sons. Highlight in your Bible: Abram, Nahor, and Haran.

Only a few generations passed between Noah and Terah. They could have known each other. Perhaps, young Terah heard Noah tell the story of the flood and God's covenant.

YOUR STORIES OF VICTORY INSPIRE OTHERS TO PURSE GOD IN RADICAL WAYS!

Genesis 11:27

Haran's son was Lot. This proves significant later.

Genesis 11:28–31

Abraham's family was from Ur of the Chaldees, which was an extremely wealthy area. The average home had 15-20 rooms. The lower level was for servants, and upper levels were for the family. There was even a chapel on their house property. These were BIG houses! Abraham had an affluent upbringing. But God was about to call Abraham to a new land that God would show him (Genesis 12:1).

Terah's son, Haran, passed away. So Terah and his remaining family journeyed away from their homes. In his heartbreak over his son's death, Terah settled. He died in a city baring the name of the son he lost. The irony of this is quiet intriguing. Verse 31 says Terah died in the place he settled. That place was named Haran, the place of his pain.

I believe Terah could have had all Abraham was about to step into, but because He held the disappointment of his son passing away, Terah was never able to move on to where God wanted to take him. In life we have to make the choice to move past the places of pain and keep going towards the future God has for us.

What disappointments have you "settled" in?

GENESIS 12

Genesis 12:1–3
After reading these verses, look at Galatians 3:29.

We are heirs to Abraham's promise which means:
1. We aren't limited to what has or has not happened in our earthly family. God has given us a new family line.
2. Greatness is in our DNA. When the disciples asked Jesus who was the greatest, Jesus did not chastise them for their question. He told them HOW to be great. (See Matthew 18:1–3 and Luke 9:46–48.) We were wired by God to desire greatness.
3. God does things *in* us to move *through* us (v. 2). What God does for you should never stop with you.
4. Every promise from God comes with sacrifice. Abraham had to make a choice. Read these verses backwards. If Abraham hadn't obeyed what God said, Abraham would never have seen verses 2 and 3 come to pass.

Genesis 12:4
Have you noticed how history comes in cycles? As you study the Bible, you'll see many children who never pushed beyond what their parents achieved. They chose to stop where their parents stopped.

However, Abraham chose to leave the place of his father's pain. Are you letting what negatively affected your parent's life stop you from moving forward?

Genesis 12:5
Everything God blessed them with was brought into their next season.

GOD NEVER WASTES ANYTHING. EVEN IN THEIR DEEPEST PAIN, GOD BLESSED THEM ABUNDANTLY.

Notice who Abraham brought with him, even though he was told exactly what to do in 12:1.

Genesis 12:6–7
Abraham passed through an area where God revealed Abraham's children would posses the land. As parents, we need to know what promises to stand on for our children.

Sweet Abraham offers a sacrifice to seal the covenant for future generations. When we give, our giving doesn't stop with us but goes on for generations to come!

Genesis 12:8
Underline Bethel. Remember this for later.

Genesis 12:10

There was a famine in the land. Sometimes we do exactly what God told us to do, and instead of things getting better, they feel worse. Abraham, who was raised in wealth and privilege, left everything to sleep in tents. The reward for his obedience to God, it seemed, was a famine. Imagine what his wife must have thought.

Have you ever doubted hearing God because when you stepped out in obedience, things got worse?

Genesis 12:11–20

I cringe every time I read this. Oh, Abraham! Why did you do that?
Be honest. Have you ever said something dumb under pressure? I know I have! At a recent event, the speaker asked me a random question in front of a large crowd. I was stunned and felt the pressure to answer so quickly that I didn't have time to think. Before I knew it, an answer came out of my mouth, and immediately the Holy Spirit convicted my heart that it was a lie.

We all make mistakes. Pride is ugly. It looks to protect itself and make us look better than we are. Yet, like Abraham, when our hearts are repentant, God takes care of us and redeems what we mess up.

GENESIS 13

Genesis 13:2
Remember we are heirs to the same promise as Abraham. Write your name in Abraham's place. That is what God says about you! What thoughts or emotions does that trigger in you?

Genesis 13:3
After his failure, Abraham traveled a direction God did not tell him to go. As a result, he ended up right back where he began. Often our failures lead us to make decisions on our own and do things God never told us to do.

Genesis 13:4
What did Abraham do?

Genesis 13:5
Who was with Abraham?

Genesis 13:5–6
Abraham and Lot were so wealthy that the land couldn't support them both at the same time! Think about how much livestock they must have had for the land to not be enough.

Genesis 13:7
When we bring people God never told us to bring along, it always causes problems. Remember who Lot was. (See Genesis 11:27.) Abraham allowed the emotional connection to justify his disobedience, and it caused trouble.

I can't tell you how many times I have hung on to relationships that God didn't want me to have, only for them to go sour and cause damage.

What relationship is God redefining in your life?

Is there anyone still with you whom God told you to let go of?

Genesis 13:9–13
Some theologians debate that if Lot had chosen the other land, God's blessing would have been on him. I disagree. God's blessing was on Abraham, not a place. The land flourished because God's hand was on Abraham's life.

When we were planting our church, I was worried about choosing the wrong location. Someone reminded me of this story. They said, "The blessing is on YOU. Wherever you choose to plant the church, God's blessing will follow." That immediately took the pressure off of my decision.

Another time I told God, "I don't want to mess up Your plan for my life." I felt God tell me, "You give yourself too much credit for what I am going to do!" From that moment on, I have trusted God to guide my steps.

Genesis 13:15–16
If you can see it, you can have it! Vision is important for your life. What do you see in your life? A strong marriage? Kids that serve God? Financial blessings? If you can see it, you can have it!

Genesis 13:17
Highlight this verse for later.

Genesis 13:18
What does Abraham do upon arrival?

You can't take giving out of the Bible. All of the people in scripture who did great things for God faithfully gave. Those who didn't do great things for God kept all their resources for themselves.

GENESIS 14

Genesis 14:1–12

The people who ruled over this land weren't God-fearing. When God calls us to take new ground, we must be willing to remove what once ruled there. For some of you that is a poverty mentality, others it may be insecurity.

What "kings" do you have to remove from the place God is calling you to?

Genesis 14:12–17

Oh how I love these verses! Let's get a few facts straight:

1. Lot was living in sin. He was not serving God.
2. God loved Abraham enough to send someone to Abraham. There was no GPS or Google Maps, yet this person knew where to go and who to tell. Think about what a miracle that was.
3. Side note: You know you are rich when you have your own army!
4. Abraham was prepared for battle BEFORE this happened (v. 14). What we do before the battle matters most.

Genesis 14:18–20

At times in the Old Testament, there are foretellings of Jesus. The foretellings are called Messianic types and shadows. Let me show you how these verses point to Jesus.

Read Hebrews 7:1–10. He comes bringing bread and wine. (See John 6:56 and Matthew 26:17–30.)

What parallels do you see between Melchizedek and Jesus?

What does Abraham give to him? (V. 20.)

Genesis 14:21–24
How much does Abraham give in verse 24?

Genesis 15

Genesis 15:1–11
God finally spoke to Abraham again. Abraham reminded God of His promise. Even though time had gone by and many battles had taken place, Abraham held on to what God had said.

God repeated the same promise that was said in Genesis 13:14–15. Abraham had made mistakes, but God remained true to what He promised.

I love verse 7. God assured Abraham that He had been with him all along. There is never a moment in our lives when God releases us from His grip.

Again, Abraham gave to God.

How have your mistakes kept you from thinking God's promises are still true for your life?

Genesis 15:6
Read Romans 4:3, 18-22. Underline in verse 20 where it says he "grew strong." God didn't choose Abraham because he was strong. God made him strong along the journey.

Genesis 15:13
God let Abraham know what was to come in Exodus 12:40.

Genesis 15:16
Remember Genesis 12:6–7? Here God gave Abraham more details to His promise for Abraham's descendants. This wasn't fulfilled until Joshua led the Israelites to the Promise Land in Joshua 24:15.

God didn't tell Abraham everything at once. He does the same with us, revealing His plan for our lives little by little.

GENESIS 16

Genesis 16:1–2

Sarah came up with her own plan to arrive at God's promise. We have all done it. We may not have allowed our husband to sleep with another woman, but we have attempted to speed up God's timeline.

I think Sarah wanted to prove she wasn't the problem in the situation.

INSECURITY CAUSES US TO MAKE POOR CHOICES.

There is nothing more difficult for a woman than struggling to get pregnant. I am sure she thought once Abraham slept with Hagar, they would discover Abraham was the barren one. To her shock, he wasn't. The situation was birthed by Sarah's attempt to outthink God. Logic never gets us to God or His promises.

God had just finished speaking to Abraham's future, and Sarah saw her present situation as God's restraint on their lives. I believe if she had heard God's Word for herself, she wouldn't have been so quick to compromise. God's Word is what sustains us in times of waiting. Second hand revelation is not enough. We need to be continually seeking God's Word for our lives.

Genesis 16:1–16
This is a type and shadow of the law (the ten commandments). For a deeper look at this, check out my study of Exodus.

GENESIS 17

Genesis 17:1
Abraham waited 13 years after having Ishmael for God to speak to him again. No doubt he had time to regret his decision. But look at how God describes him. God doesn't see us through our failures!

Genesis 17:1–27
Abraham and Sarah received brand new identities from God, symbolizing the new people they became because of His covenant. (See 2 Corinthians 5:17.)

God gave specific instructions for preparation before the promise arrived. But not only that, He also instructed Abraham on what to do with all he already had.

> ## OUR LIVES ARE A BALANCE OF CARING FOR WHAT WE HAVE WHILE PREPARING FOR WHAT IS AHEAD.

Genesis 17:24
At 99 years old, Abraham was told to do something painful. He chose to obey and cut off his flesh to received what God promised. In the same way, we must be willing to cut away the fleshly things in our lives, such as bad attitudes, anger, gossip, greed, etc.

What is God calling you to cut away?

GENESIS 18

Genesis 18:1–2
After Abraham acted in obedience, "the Lord appeared" to him. Note how many men there were. Three is a significant number in the Bible. It means divine wholeness and completeness.[4]

Genesis 18:4
Contrast this with John 13:8.

Abraham served God in action then also in giving (Genesis 18:5-9).

Genesis 18:10
After Abraham gave, God reconfirmed His covenant. The same happens every time we give: God will reconfirm the covenant on our lives.

Genesis 18:10
God had a season in mind when the promise would come. Even though Abraham was 99 years old, God still knew the perfect time to give them a baby.

---

[4]Thompson, Adam F., Beale, Adrian. *The Divinity Code to Understanding Your Dreams and Visions.* Destiny Image: December 2011.

YOUR APPOINTED SEASON IS COMING WHEN GOD WANTS TO GIVE YOU EVERYTHING HE HAS PROMISED.

Genesis 18:12–15
Sarah's response wasn't bad; it was a reflection of her heart at the time. Often, we say we are believing for something, but the deep recesses of our heart show what we truly believe. See Luke 5:22.

Genesis 18:17
I love this verse so much! God calls you His friend. Think about that!

Genesis 18:18
God reminded Abraham of Genesis 12:1–3. God's Word always confirms His Word.

Genesis 18:19, 23–33
God always does something in our lives to help others. Here Abraham interceded for his family.

Lot had been rescued once before, but he found himself in trouble again. God's grace rescued him. Aren't you thankful that God doesn't have a limited amount of mercy in our lives?

GENESIS 19

Genesis 19:1–3
Even though Lot was in sin, he recognized God's
presence. I think of him being a young boy hearing
the stories of his uncle's encounters with the Lord.
Many years had gone by, but Lot still had a
reverential fear of the Lord. (See Isaiah 55:11.)

Patterning after what he had seen his uncle do, Lot
gave a sacrifice.

Genesis 19:4–11
These verses are sickening. They show how far the
people were from God.

Genesis 19:12–16
The angels asked about his household. Again, we see
God's concern for our families.

Genesis 19:17
God's instructions are always to protect us, not to
keep us from things. Each instruction has a purpose.
When we disobey those instructions, we are often left
with sad consequences.

Genesis 19:27
Note what time Abraham went up. (See Mark 1:35,
Psalm 119:147, and Matthew 6:33.)

Genesis 19:29

Have you heard the saying, "If God had a refrigerator, your picture would be on it." I love that this verse tells us that we are imprinted on His mind.[5]

Genesis 19:30–38

So sad. No matter how many chances Lot had, he kept making poor life choices. I often wonder if the loss of his father at a young age started his search for happiness and fulfillment. We will never know what it was. Yet, Abraham loved him.

Underline the name Moab (v. 37). Moab is significant because Deuteronomy 23:3 tells us that God forbade Moabites to enter the presence of God. Ruth was a Moabite (see Ruth 1:2), and yet she served the Lord. In upcoming chapters of Genesis, the twelves tribes of Israel are formed, but alongside them were groups of people, like the Moabites, who lived wickedly in the sight of the Lord and their families served other gods.

Remember, the choices you make today will effect generations to come.

---

[5] *AMPC*

GENESIS 20

Genesis 20:1–18

Why Abraham chose to move again is unknown. God didn't direct him to do so. Maybe Lot's bad choices broke his heart so he moved away. Maybe the unsettledness of waiting for the promise of God drove him. Whatever the reason, he put himself in a situation where he made some terrible choices. Again. And again God gets Abraham out of trouble.

I often wonder how Sarah felt being given to other men. I am sure that bred a lot of her insecurity.

This chapter leaves me wondering why Abraham continually made mistakes yet New Testament scripture recorded the opposite of what we see here. Read Hebrews 11:8–12 and take note of how the Bible talks about Abraham. From studying his life, do you feel like these verses recorded the good parts or the bad parts of his journey?

I AM THANKFUL THAT
WHEN GOD LOOKS OVER
MY LIFE HE REMEMBERS
THE GOOD I HAVE DONE
AND NOT THE BAD.

GENESIS 21

Genesis 21:1
I love this verse. You can almost jump over it if you aren't careful.

Let's highlight two things:
> 1. The Lord visited Sarah. One moment with God changes everything!
> 2. "The Lord did for her as He promised." God is faithful to keep His promises!

What promises are you still believing for?

Genesis 21:3–6
Isaac's name came from Genesis 18:13–16. Sarah never stopped laughing. God's promises bring a special joy to our lives that we wouldn't normally have.

Genesis 21:8

This reminds me to celebrate and enjoy every season. It is beautiful how intentional Abraham was about celebrating the small things in Isaac's life.

Are you taking time to celebrate your small steps of progress?

Genesis 21:9–20

There is a lot to take in from these verses, but I want you to see the type and shadow of what is birthed out of flesh versus out of promise.

Read Galatians 4:21–31.

Here are the contrasts I want you to see:
•What we do out of our flesh vs. God's supernatural help
•Works of the flesh vs. works of the spirit
•The law (man's attempt to get to God) vs. Jesus (God's journey to us)
•Hagar represents the spiritual enslavement that happens when we try to keep the law. Isaac represents

the freedom we have in trusting Jesus. (See Galatians 5:1.)

What in your life represents Ishmael (acts of the flesh) and what represents Isaac (trust in God's promise)?

Concept Chart		
MOTHER	Sarah	Hagar
HER STATUS	Free	Slave
HER SON	Isaac	Ishmael
HIS STATUS	Persecuted	Persecutor
BORN BY	Promise	Flesh
COVENANT	Gospel	The Law
MEDIATOR	Jesus [God]	Moses [Man]
INHERITANCE	Heaven	Jerusalem
CULMINATION	Established	Abolished

Genesis 21:16–17
Notice how tender God was to the cries of a woman before women were really seen and heard.

Even though Abraham made mistakes with her and Sarah despised her, God still cared for Hagar.

Genesis 21:22
Oh that people would say this of us.

Genesis 21:23–34
They argued over the well of water. Pay attention to how much this happens in the Bible. At that time, whoever controlled the water source also controlled the city.
Water is symbolic of two things in the Bible:
1. The Word of God
2. The Holy Spirit

If we want God to take over our cities, it will be through the Word of God and the Holy Spirit.

Genesis 21:31
Underline Beersheba. We will revisit this later.

GENESIS 22

This chapter is full of symbolic meanings. For the purposes of this study, we won't be able to fully cover them all, but I will do my best to point them out and help you understand them.

Genesis 22:1
After we receive a blessing from God, testing always follows. For example, every week when we get paid, are we going to give back to God what is His or are we going to keep it all for ourselves? God gives us what we ask for, then examines our hearts and actions to see if we love what He gave us more than we love Him.

Genesis 22:2
Many years passed, but the command stayed the same. Read Genesis 12:1.

> ## OUR JOURNEY HAS AND ALWAYS WILL BE BY FAITH, TRUSTING GOD TO SHOW US THE NEXT STEP.

God led Abraham out of Haran by faith, and years later, his next journey still took faith. One required faith to go and receive. The next required faith and trust in what God had already given.

Remember in Genesis 18:24–33 when Abraham interceded for God's salvation if 10 righteous people could be found in the city. No doubt Abraham remembered what happened with Lot after those events. Here in chapter 22, the number of people in need of salvation was narrowed down to one, his only son, yet he continued to walk in obedience of what God asked of him.

Obedience is never easy, but it is always worth it.

What areas has God been stretching your obedience in?

Genesis 22:5
Abraham didn't know what was about to happen, but he knew that his obedience was worship to God. (See 1 Samuel 15:22.) Every step Abraham took up the mountain was like a statement of faith that God was going to make a way.

Genesis 22:6–12
This scripture is symbolic of another man who would carry wood up the side of a mountain, but for him,

there wouldn't be a replacement sacrifice. He would have to lay down His life.

Read John 19:7, Revelation 13:8, and Hebrews 11:17–19.

The act of Abraham giving his son, Isaac, paved the way so God could later give His Son, Jesus. Whatever we bind on Earth is bound in Heaven and whatever we release on Earth is released in Heaven (Matthew 18:18). Abraham couldn't have fully understood what his obedience did. Our simple acts of obedience are more significant than we realize.

Anything God asks of us is to reveal the intention our heart. He is never after the physical thing He asks for. His true treasure is our heart.

What about you? When have you obeyed God, only to later realize the bigger impact those acts of obedience had on your life? Take a moment to write about them.

Genesis 22:12–18

Immediately after Abraham's obedience, God pronounced a blessing. If God isn't moving in your life, then go back to the last thing He told you to do and do it!

Read Hebrews 6:13–20.

Genesis 22:19

Notice where Abraham went. Remember when I told you to underline this place? Who lives there? (Hint Genesis 21:14.) I will address this more in the next chapter.

GENESIS 23

Genesis 23:1
Sarah died when Isaac was 37 years old. After a long and difficult life of faith, she went to Heaven.
Job lived more of his life after tragedy happened than before it. Noah was the same way. But Sarah believed God for a child until she was past 90 years old, then for 37 years she lived in the fulfillment of what God promised her.

Genesis 23:2–4
Verse 2 says Abraham went to mourn Sarah, implying that they did not live together when she died. Then in verses 3–4, Abraham called himself a stranger to the people of the area. Remember where Abraham moved after the sacrifice of Isaac (Genesis 22:19). From the text we can presume that after Abraham attempted to sacrifice Isaac, Sarah and Isaac left to dwell in Kiriath-arba without him. Can you blame her? She had followed Abraham all over the country, been given to other men twice, and nearly lost her son. She finally had enough.

> ### OBEDIENCE SOMETIMES MEANS THE CLOSEST PEOPLE TO YOU MIGHT REJECT YOU.

Genesis 23:5–20

After years of moving and traveling, Abraham finally gave Sarah a place to rest. This final act of love is endearing. Perhaps he was attempting to make up for years that were lost.

In verse 11, the people tried to give Abraham the land, but Abraham refused the free gift. Instead, he paid the equivalent of $128,000 today for her burial place (v. 15).

Sarah's body was placed in a cave (v. 19). Abraham ensured her burial would honor the life she lived. Later Abraham, Isaac, Rebekah, Jacob, and Leah were buried there. Rachel was the only one who wasn't. That is a story for later.

GENESIS 24

Genesis 24:1
Notice how much God blessed Abraham.

Genesis 24:2–10
Do you remember who this is?
See Genesis 15:2.

Before his children were born, Eliezer was the closest
thing Abraham had to a son, and here he trusted
Eliezer to bring Isaac a wife. Life comes full circle if
you wait long enough. Be careful how you treat
people. You never know what your next chapter could
hold and how you might need them!
Notice how detailed Abraham's instructions were. As
leaders, we must give clear direction for the people we
are leading.

After Sarah died, Abraham seemed urgent to give
Isaac a wife. As we've seen, Isaac lived with his mother
and was close with her. Probably even closer than he
was to his father. Abraham wanted to relieve his son's
grieving heart. Abraham had loved Sarah so deeply,
that finding similar love and happiness for his son
seemed like the best gift he could give Isaac.

Genesis 24:12–14

Eliezer's prayer was specific and honoring. He knew his task couldn't be done without God's help. How many things do we attempt to do without relying on help from God? God can do more with our five minutes of prayer than we can in five hours of work on our own.

Genesis 24:15–27

Rebekah had no idea her act of service was about to give her a blessing without measure. Watering 10 camels was a huge task. To put this in perspective, one camel can drink 53 gallons in 3 minutes. She had 10 camels to water. I'll let you do the math. Keep in mind there wasn't a hose to get the job done. She had to use what she had: a bucket making trip after trip back and forth to the well.

One of my favorite quotes is, "The greatest test of a servant is when you are treated like one."

See Matthew 23:11.

Her act is inspiring to me! I have a hard time washing dishes when people are sitting on the couch! I can't imagine performing her task with a clean heart. In the same way God was after Abraham's heart in his willingness to sacrifice Isaac, God was after Rebekah's heart. And He is after our heart.

Those camels were more than just camels. They held the promise of financial wealth and a husband meant for her, but it hinged on her obedience. If she had not been willing to serve, she would have only returned home with water for her family and nothing else. How many blessings do we miss because our pride gets in the way?

How hard is it for you to be treated like a servant?

Genesis 24:29–52
Pay attention to the brother's name. He becomes important later.

The servant only did what his master sent him to do and only said what his master told him to say. He didn't give his opinion. We must be careful to follow what God has told us to do and say. When we obey, we will get what we desire.

Genesis 24:54–58
These verses reveal Laban's character. Remember this for later.

Genesis 24:63–67

These verses are so sweet. Isaac was in prayer for his wife. Verse 67 lets us know that she helped comfort him after his mother's death.

Genesis 25:1
Remember, we talked about Beersheba earlier. Note that Abraham took another wife. Many theologians would say that her name was changed but that she was Hagar.

Genesis 25:5
How much did Abraham give Isaac?

How do you think Hagar felt about that?

Genesis 25:7
Isaac was 75 years old when his father passed away.

Genesis 25:8
Underline the description of Abraham when he died. Read Psalm 91:16.

God promises us that we don't have to die until we are satisfied. So that means if you aren't satisfied, then God isn't done!

Genesis 25:9–11
These verses always make me cry. The two sons came together to honor their dad. They traveled to the place where Sarah had been buried over 30 years before. Abraham's body was reunited with Sarah. Even at the end of his life, God fulfilled Abraham's deep longing: everyone together and at peace. I wonder how Hagar felt as they placed Abraham in the cave with Sarah, knowing she would never be reunited with him again and that Sarah got the final say after all.

Genesis 25:16
Ishmael had 12 princes. God was about to birth 12 tribes out of Isaac's son, Jacob (Israel). The enemy always presents something resembling what God is about to do, but it is always counterfeit for the real thing. In the same way Ishmael came before the promised child (Isaac), these 12 princes came before the 12 tribes. Out of these 12 princes came much of the civil unrest we still see today.

Genesis 25:19–26
Pay attention to how the children were born. They wrestled in the womb, at birth, and as children.

Genesis 25:27–34

Have you ever compromised on something but later regretted it?

How was Esau's compromise similar to what Abraham carried out with Hagar?

GENESIS 26

This is the only chapter that focuses on Isaac.

Genesis 26:1
Do you remember King Abimelech? Go back and
read Genesis 21:22–32.

A famine forced them out of Canaan into the land of
the Philistines.

Genesis 26:2–5
God assured Isaac the blessing of Abraham was also
on his life. I am sure he had moments when he
wondered if God would be with him the same way
God was with his dad. We do the same thing. We
have no trouble believing God will do something for
someone else, but when it comes to faith for our own
life, we struggle.

In verse 5, God spoke about Abraham's obedience.
Do you think of Abraham in this way?

I love the saying, "God measures our faithfulness in years and not days." We all have bad days, but God looks for the theme of our lives to be obedience and faithfulness (v. 5). Will we make mistakes? Yes. Are we going to fall short? Yes. His grace is big enough. We choose to keep seeking what He has for our lives.

How do you feel knowing God looks over your life and sees the good not the bad you have done?

Genesis 26:6–11

Does this story sound familiar? I cringe reading that Isaac repeated what his father did years before. Isaac wasn't even alive when Abraham treated Sarah this way. In parenting, we reproduce who we are, not who we aspire to be.

God chooses us, even in our frailty. He knows we will make mistakes. Remember, Abraham made this mistake twice, and Isaac did only once. This is a type and a shadow pointing to when Peter denied Christ three times, and God still used him. (See John 18:13–27.)

Genesis 26:12

In the midst of famine, Isaac sowed seed. I've heard the quote, "If what you have can't fill your need; then it is seed to sow!" That must have been Isaac's philosophy. I am sure he felt a lot of pressure to care for his young sons, Jacob and Esau, yet he continued to sow seed knowing that it would bring about the harvest and the blessing.

Read this again through the eyes of Jacob as a child. Notice what he saw his father doing and how these actions impacted his own actions later in his life.

How does what you saw a child change the way you see:
- Relationships?
- God?
- Opportunities?

Genesis 26:13–14

God fulfilled what He promised to Isaac in verses 2–5. In the natural, the logical decision was for him to take refuge in the wealthy country of Egypt, but Isaac obeyed God. Our obedience always opens the door of God's provision.

Genesis 26:15–22

At that time, whoever controlled the water source controlled the region. I love that God fulfilled His promise, but Isaac still had to provide water to the people around him! Water in the Bible is symbolic of the Word of God and the Holy Spirit.

The enemy tries to stop our wells any way he can: through offense, busy schedules, wrong thinking, etc. We will only fulfill our calling if we take control over the wells in our life.

Isaac finished what Abraham had started. (See Genesis 12:7, Genesis 13:17–18, and Genesis 21:22–30.)

GOD ALWAYS FINISHES WHAT HE STARTS.

You may not see it in your lifetime, but eventually, He will complete it! You can rest assured that He is faithful to do what He has said.

Genesis 26:26–31
In verse 16, Abimelech asked Isaac to leave, but the king returns humbled by what he has seen God do for Isaac. Eventually, even the people who don't like you, will have to acknowledge God's hand on your life!

Genesis 26:34–35
Some say that Esau's downhill journey began when he lost his father's blessing in the next chapter. However, I believe when he surrendered his birthright in chapter 25, the blessing of God lifted off his life. But

if it wasn't the stew, it would have been something else. These verses show he was a person of compromise from the beginning. He made choices that caused trouble in the family.

GENESIS 27

Genesis 27:1–29

What a paradox that Esau forfeited his birthright when he returned from hunting, then later lost his blessing when he left to hunt.

Jacob didn't question his mother. He went along with her plan and did as he was told, taking on the identity of another person to get what he wanted.

Remember in Genesis 26 when Isaac deceived Abimelech to get what he wanted? Jacob was a young child watching this transaction, and now grown, he did the same thing, except to own his father. He played the part skillfully in verse 20, saying God blessed him with the hunt. However, in actuality, his mother prepared the food (v. 17).

Lies have a way of snowballing, don't they? Something small turns into something big quickly.

Genesis 27:30–42

Truth has a way of coming to the forefront. I can't imagine Esau's sadness. He had made poor choices, but the rejection he felt was real. His mother had ensured he didn't receive his father's blessing.

The Bible tells us that Esau was a strong man and Jacob dwelt in tents (Genesis 25:27). Since Esau was outdoors often, the bond between Jacob and his mother was stronger. After all, Jacob was inside with her when Esau would go away for long trips. As a parent, you aren't supposed to have favorites, but clearly, Jacob was Rebekah's favorite. So when she saw Esau's anger, she wanted to protect Jacob.

Genesis 27:43–45

Rebekah gave Jacob specific instructions on where and how to flee from Esau's anger. For the first time, Jacob was about to go into the wilderness. Alone. The son she loved the most was about to be in God's hands.

Her words pierce my heart, "Why should I be deprived of you both in a single day?" Little did she know, she would never see Jacob again.

Compromise never gets us what we want. It didn't work for Adam compromising to make Eve happy or Moses striking a rock to make the Israelites stop complaining. In the end, you never get what you want.

Neither Rebekah nor Jacob knew that these would be the last times they would see each other.

GENESIS 28

Genesis 28:1–10

The blessing was an outward sign of the inward condition of their hearts. Compare the actions of Esau and Jacob.

Consider how bitterness and rejection caused Esau to do the opposite of what he should have.

Take a moment to write your thoughts about Jacob.

Life is a series of small choices we make. The big moments are not what change the trajectory of our lives. It is the little steps we make along the way that get us where we are.

Genesis 28:11–16

When Jacob was alone, he had his own encounter with God. I love that God appeared to Jacob in a place of rest. All his life, Jacob had to work and strive, but in God, he only had to rest to receive a blessing.

Notice God did not rebuke Jacob for his mistakes. He only spoke to Jacob's potential.

Genesis 28:16
This verse grips my heart. May we always be aware of God's presence.

Genesis 28:18–22
These are important verses. Remember the name of this place. It will be significant later.

GENESIS 29

Genesis 29:1
God's presence renews our joy and endurance. After being in the presence of God, Jacob made a 400 mile journey with joy and ease.

Read Psalm 16:11 and Isaiah 40:31.

Genesis 29:2–11
After traveling so far, what relief he must have felt when he found his mother's people. It was love at first sight when Jacob saw Rachel. This begins my favorite love story in the Bible.

Genesis 29:12–28
God forgives us the moment we ask, but what we have sown we will still eventually reap. Laban deceived Jacob, the same way Jacob had deceived his own father.

Genesis 29:29–Genesis 30:24
These verses introduce the children who become the 12 tribes of Israel. They are significant. Each child's purpose was far greater than they realized. Underline their names to reference later in our study. Note who each of their mothers were.

Genesis 30:24
Whose son was Joseph? Oh how she waited for him.

Genesis 30:25–43
Underline Jacob's desire to leave in verse 25.
No matter how many times Laban tried to trick and deceive him, God blessed Jacob. In the same way God was with his father and grandfather, He was with Jacob.

Take a moment to think about times people have tried to harm you but God protected you.

GENESIS 31

Genesis 31:1–4
Notice how in Genesis 30:25 Jacob was ready to leave Laban's house, but God hadn't told them to leave yet. We must be willing to stay in place until God releases us. In verse 3 of this chapter, God directed Jacob where to go and promised to be with him.

Genesis 31:7
Jacob knew the source of his blessing. God's hand of protection had blessed him.

Genesis 31:10–13
Jacob had a second dream where God spoke to him. (The first was in Genesis 28:12–16.) One of his sons would also have dreams that would impact a nation.

Genesis 31:13
Who does God refer to Himself as?

Why do you think God called Himself that?

Genesis 31:14

Greed causes us to do foolish things. Jacob was extremely wealthy. Therefore, Rachel lacked nothing, but inside she wanted more. That greed would later cost her everything.

Genesis 31:14–17

After God told Jacob to leave, he talked it over with Leah and Rachel (v. 4). Jacob had stayed in their father's home hoping to receiving a blessing from Laban. Maybe it was because the only blessing he had ever received was through deception that he wanted a new blessing through hard work and honesty. Or perhaps he was like many of us and just wanted Laban to like him. In verse 16, we hear Rachel and Leah's frustration as they urged Jacob to take action! Finally, in verse 17, Jacob released his need for Laban's approval and stepped into what God told him to do.

Whose approval are you waiting for? How has it stopped you from doing what God has asked of you?

Genesis 31:19–32

All Jacob knew how to do was run away. He ran from Esau years before, and he ran away from Laban instead of facing the situation. Had he been honest with Laban instead, I wonder if the story would have turned out differently. Maybe he wouldn't have lost Rachel.

When Laban caught up to him, Jacob revealed why he ran (v. 31). Fear always makes decisions that we regret later.

What decisions have you made out of fear that you regretted?

Genesis 31:34–55

Rachel lied to Laban about why she could not stand up. She concealed what she had stolen. So many lies. So much deceit.

Laban and Jacob finally had a conversation that should have happened years ago. They found common ground and made covenant with one another. However, Jacob was about to have another difficult conversation.

We must get our hearts right before we can receive what God has for us next.

How many conversations have you been avoiding?

GENESIS 32

Genesis 32:1
Anywhere God calls us, we are never alone or on our own.
Read John 14:3 and Psalm 23:6.

Genesis 32:6
Remember that Joseph was a young boy watching how his father handled conflict. This will be important later when we read about Joseph.

Genesis 32:7–12
How often do we pray for the best but prepare for the worst?

Genesis 32:13–32
Jacob sent everything he had ahead of him: his gifts and his family. How often do we do this? We put our gifts, talents, abilities, and our family ahead of us. We give it all for the acceptance of people.

Jacob didn't know who he was. His family tried to tell him who he was. He tried to find his identity in outward things. But in the stillness of the night, when he was stripped down from all he identified himself as, God found him. That is how God wants to find us. In our rawest form. That is when we find out who we are. When we are not hiding behind our talents or our family.

This was so much more than a name change. Jacob's name signified his identity with past mistakes. With a new name, God erased all the wrong Jacob done.

Read 2 Corinthians 5:17.

How often do you hide behind your schedule, family, or gifts?

When is the last time you got quiet before the Lord?

GENESIS 33

Genesis 33:1

Immediately, he saw his brother coming. I am sure dread overwhelmed him. He was walking with a limp after wrestling with God, which meant he had to approach his brother with an obvious weakness instead of perceived strength.

Read 2 Corinthians 12:9–11.

Genesis 33:2

Notice who was in the front and who was at the very back.

Genesis 33:3–4

Note the similarity of Esau's response to the story in Luke 15:20–24. Total forgiveness. No bitterness or resentment for the wrongs committed. All those years, Jacob lived in shame. I think he put up with Laban's corruption for so long because of the shame he held over what happened with Esau.

Are you carrying the shame of relationships from your past?

Genesis 33:5
Jacob was wealthy and successful, yet who did he refer
to himself as?

Genesis 33:7
Young Joseph bowed before the uncle his father had
wronged years before. His face bowed low to the dirt,
trembling beside his mother. They had lived in fear of
this moment. Then he witnessed the beautiful
exchange of two brothers reconciling their differences.
This moment defined him for the rest of his life.

Genesis 33:9–16
We will never know why Jacob gave a bogus reason
for not going with Esau. He promised his brother to
eventually catch up, but he never did. The deceiver
was still deceiving. He never saw Esau again.

Genesis 33:17–20
Jacob moved to Succoth, in the opposite direction of
his brother. This was only supposed to be a temporary
stopping place, but Jacob stayed for many years.
This was a violation of the promise he made to God
to return to Bethel. (See Genesis 28:15.)

God's people were forbidden to live among those who weren't of faith (see Genesis 28:6), and yet here Jacob settled in Canaan among them.

Note the names of the men with whom Jacob did business.

The altar Jacob built in verse 20 is his partial obedience to what he promised to God. Settling here and building an altar was more convenient than journeying the full distance.

PARTIAL OBEDIENCE IS STILL DISOBEDIENCE.

Before continuing, I want you to know that God is full of grace. However, when we make choices to disobey, we remove ourselves from His protection. God fully forgives us when we fail, but sometimes the price of our mistakes is irreversible. The next chapter is difficult, and I want you emotionally prepared for it before we move on.

GENESIS 34

Genesis 34:1

Women were never supposed to travel alone. They were thought to be helpless without male protection, so traveling alone was considered too dangerous. Insecure Leah had Dinah, a daughter who was strong and confident. Leah lived her entire life in fear of what men thought of her, and Dinah moved about the country confidently. (My book, *Happily Even After*, is written about Leah with a whole chapter devoted to Dinah. You can purchase a copy on Amazon.)

Genesis 34:2–4

The progression of verse 2 in *The Amplified Bible* is heartbreaking. "Humbled, defiled and disgraced."[6]

Humble—showing a low estimate of ones importance or value
Defiled—to make unclean, violate, and corrupt the purity of
Disgraced—humiliate, source of shame, or lose favor[7]

---

[6] AMPC
[7] "humble," "defile," "disgrace." *Merriam-Webster.com.* 2019. https://www.merriam-webster.com (May 2019).

Here Dinah was the picture of confidence. Some commentaries say the journey she took in verse one was to speak to women, empowering them in their value and worth. Others say that she was curious to see the culture of the women in the area. I like to believe she went to make a difference. If it was dangerous for women to travel alone, curiosity of culture was not worth risking one's life. I believe she had a deeper cause for her actions. Her confidence to travel alone in a land that she didn't know is inspiring.

However, verse two changed her. She lost her sense of value, her purity, and she took on shame for what was done to her.

What about you? How have you let someone else's actions change the way you see yourself?

Genesis 34:5–24
Jacob was used to running and not facing his problems. Before it was his brother and Laban. But this was his daughter. His silence was deafening.

Thankfully, Dinah's brothers knew Jacob was wrong. I am certain Leah and Rachel advocated for Dinah's safe return. Not only was Shechem an awful person for what he had done, but he was also from the land where Jacob was forbidden.

> # WHEN GOD TELLS US TO DEAL WITH THINGS, WE MUST DEAL WITH THEM IN THEIR ENTIRETY OR ELSE THEY WILL APPEAR IN ANOTHER SEASON OF LIFE.

Jacob thought he had gotten away with his partial obedience to God (Genesis 33:19–20). In his disobedience, he made peace with the very enemy who later hurt his daughter.

Jacob's sons devised a plan to rescue their sister. Remember Joseph was one of Dinah's brothers. He was a young boy at the time but attentively watched the way his brothers defended his sister.

Genesis 34:25–29
It is unknown how long Dinah waited for help. We are not told what was done to her while she waited, but I can imagine the relief she felt when she heard her brothers battling in the city. Simeon and Levi, Dinah's full brothers, were only young men and

seemingly insignificant threats, yet they overtook an entire city.

Genesis 34:30–31
Jacob's selfish nature came to the forefront again. He was more concerned with his neighbors approving of him. (Keep in mind, these were people God forbade him to live with or allow his family to marry.) His sons' response in verse 31 is heartbreaking. I wonder if Dinah overheard this argument.

GENESIS 35

Genesis 35:1
God's grace is unlimited. Again he appeared to Jacob and reminded him of where he should be. He didn't address Jacob's failures. God only points to our potential.

Genesis 35:2–4
Jacob's household prepared for the journey to Bethel. Jacob knew they needed to get rid of their gods and idols, yet he buried them instead of destroying them. Just in case they needed them later. Then they changed their clothes before the journey. Funny how we change outwardly visible things in an attempt to get away with our disobedience.

Read Matthew 23:27–28.

If we aren't careful, we will be just like Jacob's house (and the scribes and Pharisees of the New Testament) changing the outside and not taking care of our heart. We still do this today. We focus on our actions, clothing, and behaviors forgetting that it is our beliefs that change our actions and desires. Wrong believing will always result in wrong living. Are you spending more of your time trying to change what people see or are you allowing God to change your heart?

Take a moment to write your thoughts.

Genesis 35:5
Even though Jacob's household was still dealing with
disobedience in areas of their lives, God's hand of
blessing was on them. The enemy is fearful of what is
blessed by God.

In your lowest moments, you still represent Jesus in
the spiritual realm. Your disobedience does not
disqualify you from the blessing and the call of God
on your life. (See Romans 11:29–32.)

Genesis 35:6–7
Jacob fulfilled the promise he made to God as a
youth.

Genesis 35:8
When Jacob fled from Esau, he never saw his mother
again. Somewhere along the way, he was reunited
with Rebekah's nurse. She was the closest thing that
he had to his mom. Now, she was gone too.

Genesis 35:9–15
God showed up in the midst of his pain and
reminded him of His promise. God reminded him
that he was no longer Jacob, but he was now Israel.

What do you think that means?

Genesis 35:16–20
They set out in obedience to God, and along the way,
Rachel went into labor with Benjamin. In an
agonizing childbirth, she died. The woman Jacob had
spent 14 years praying for and had loved so deeply
was gone.

Genesis 35:21
Jacob spent years running away, but pain had
followed him everywhere he went. Until he came
face-to-face with who God had called him to be.
In verse 20, he was Jacob. Then in verse 21, after he
stepped into his calling, he's called Israel.

Genesis 35:22–29
When the Bible described Isaac at the end of his life, what did it say? Read Psalm 91. What kind of life are we promised to have?

Esau and Jacob saw each other again to bury their father. They were young boys when Isaac and Ishmael buried Abraham. Now they too reunited for Isaac's burial. This was the last time they ever saw each other.

GENESIS 36

Esau lived his life opposite of what God wanted for His people, including but not limited to marrying ungodly women (See Genesis 27:46). In this chapter, two nations began to form. Esau's descendants (the Edomites) warred against Israel for generations to come. Moses came up against the Edomites in Numbers 20:14–21. Saul fought the Edomites in 1 Samuel 14:47.

The Edomites are referenced many times throughout the Bible, but one is especially interesting. At the birth of Jesus, King Herod declared the death of all male children under the age of two. Herod was a descendent of Esau, an Edomite.

Let's read this excerpt out of commentary:

> Personally I have seen the pattern and ambiguities of Esau's chronicle traced in the lives of men I have buried over the years. They were born to godly, though imperfect, parents. Growing up, they were nurtured and catechized in God's Word. But Christian things meant little to them. Heaven was far-off, disconnected from real life. And as they matured, they came to despise their heritage—

maybe not overtly but by neglect and dismissiveness. Some were ignorant despisers, others cultured despisers.

To their parents' great sorrow, they married outside the faith and then went with the flow of culture in raising their children so that they became *de facto* pagans pursuing and even attaining the American dream.

But as these men passed through midlife, the emptiness of it all began to pummel their souls. They repented and came to faith. When they could, they made amends. But their families did not follow. So these men stayed at the fringes of the church, sometimes seeking counsel, engaging in benevolences, attending irregularly and alone, inarticulate as to their faith.

When they died, the family asked for a funeral in the church in respect to their father's wishes. And when I preached, it was to ignorant, unbelieving hearts—Edomites.[8]

---

[8] Hughes, R. K. (2004). *Genesis: beginning and blessing* (p. 431). Wheaton, IL: Crossway Books.

What can you learn from Esau's choices and family history?

What can you do today to ensure your family history isn't like Esau's?

GENESIS 37

This chapter includes the ninth lineage written in Genesis but is by far the most extensive of them all. Esau's family line was mostly summed up in one chapter. However, Moses, the author of Genesis, spent 13 chapters explaining the lineage of Jacob (Israel). This story takes us from the pastures of Palestine to the palace of kings to the depths of a prison. Perhaps Moses spent so much time on the story of Joseph because this ultimately led Israel into bondage for 400 years in Egypt. Whatever the reason, Joseph's story is one of redemption, forgiveness, and grace.

There is much foreshadowing of Jesus in Joseph's life. (See Isaiah 53:3 and John 1:11.)

Take notice each time the Bible uses the name Jacob (deceiver) and Israel (new identity). There is rich symbolism as he operates out of his old sin nature and his new identity in God.

Genesis 37:2-4
Joseph was kept separate from his other brothers, yet he was with Bilhah and Zilpah. If you remember Bilhah was who committed incest with Ruben (Leah's first son) in Genesis 35:22. I find it precarious that

Jacob wanted to protect his son yet didn't carefully select who spent time with him.

Jacob was unquestionably partial toward Joseph. The coat of many colors was extremely expensive. This would be like your parent's giving you a Mercedes Benz while your siblings received a Kia Sol. His brothers weren't just upset that Joseph tattled on them, but that he did so clothed in his father's favor.

Some commentaries say the coat of colors was given because Joseph told on his brothers. Others say Joseph received it at a younger age.

Genesis 37:5–9
When people already don't like you, they will despise even more when you announce God's plan for your life.

This dream was prophetic of what was to come in Joseph's life. All throughout the Bible, God used dreams to talk to His people, and He still does today.

Genesis 37:10–11
Jacob's neglect and attempts to avoid conflict hurt so many people, including his children.

Genesis 37:12
The specifics of what Joseph knew about his brothers was left unsaid in verse 2, but verse 12 hinted to what

they might have been doing. Do you recognize where they went and remember what happened there? Look back at Genesis 35:4.

REMEMBER, WHAT WE DON'T DEAL WITH WILL ULTIMATELY DEAL WITH US.

The boys were young children when they watched their father bury the idols and other gods. Now in their adulthood, they returned to those gods, while Jacob looked the other way.

We can't know everything as parents, but as soon as God makes us aware of an issue, our job is to confront it.

Genesis 37:13–35
There is so much to see in these verses.
Who stood up for Joseph in verse 21? Reuben was Leah's first born child. He didn't have access to his birthright because of what was done with Bilhah. He was the only one with nothing to gain from getting rid of Joseph yet he was the one who spoke up. Experiencing failure and learning from it makes us respond to circumstances differently.

There was no water in the pit where they put Joseph (v. 24). Water is symbolic of the word and the Holy Spirit.

What deeper meaning do you think that holds?

The brothers sold Joseph for 20 pieces of silver which was the equivalent of $400. Split among 11 brothers, it would be a little over $36 each. They did not need the money, being that their father was extremely wealthy. But it was never about the money; it was a way of erasing their problem. They followed the example of what their father had done all their lives. They ran away from the issue instead of dealing with the real issue: their hearts.

Generations later, another man would be sold for 30 pieces of silver by a person trying to erase a problem instead of dealing with his heart issue. (See Matthew 26:15.)

Verse 31 is painfully reminiscent of another time clothing was dipped in blood to get the blessing of a father. (See Genesis 27:11–27.) Jacob came full circle. The deceiver raised kids who then deceived him. What he had done in the tent as a child followed him into a field in his old age with his sons. All for one thing: a father's approval.

Genesis 37:34

I wonder what went through Jacob's mind when they told him. Was he faced with regret? Did the wrong committed against Dinah flash through his mind? Did a longing for Rachel pull at his heart? Whatever his emotions were, this is the first time we witness deep hurt in Jacob.

Genesis 37:35

Oh this makes me cry, "His sons and daughters attempted to console him."
Dinah had wept alone for the wrong done to her. Scripture does not show a single instance when her father defended or comforted her. Yet here she stood by his side in his pain.

How well do you give to others what you wish you would have gotten?

Genesis 37:36

Jacob's mistakes came back to haunt him, but there were remnants of Abraham's mistakes as well. Joseph was sold to the Midianites, who were descendants of Ishmael.

GENESIS 38

Genesis 38:1–30
This chapter could be confusing so let me break it
down.

Judah knew the warnings from Abraham, Isaac, and
Jacob about marrying Canaanite women. He was the
fourth born son and heir to his father's inheritance
due to the mistakes of his elder brothers. Yet he began
making his own mistakes.

Judah met and married a woman who Scripture left
nameless. All we know of her was that she was the
daughter of Shua. They had three sons: Er, Onan,
and Shelah. Er took Tamar as his wife. Then Er died
because of his wickedness. Judah gave Tamar to Onan
in marriage, but Onan died. Then Judah asked Tamar
to stick around until his youngest was old enough to
marry. But Tamar devised her own plan.

She removed the clothing that identified her as a
widow, disguised herself as a prostitute, then found
her father-in-law. What she asked for as payment was
sure to identify her as the prostitute later and would
get her out of trouble. In other words, she set him up
and blackmailed him.

Tamar became pregnant by Judah and had twins: Perez and Zerah.

Compare this with Luke 3:33, Genesis 25:24–26.

Tamar was the first of the five women listed in Jesus' lineage. (See Matthew 1:1–9.)

Read Ephesians 2:11–13 and Matthew 15:22–28.

What are your thoughts on the above scriptures?

GENESIS 39

Genesis 39:1–6
Last time we saw Joseph, there were no signs of hope
for him. He was in an empty pit stripped of all he had
then sold into slavery. Now he's found his way back
into the story of Genesis. Verse 2 grips my heart every
time I read it. God was with Joseph. Those words
alone are a starting point of hope. Those four words
defined the next part of Joseph's story. Even though
he had been abandoned by his brothers and hurt by
rejection, God never left him. The same way the
presence of God was strong in his ancestor's lives, it
was also strong in his. (See Genesis 21:22, 26:27.)
Even being a slave couldn't stop God's big plan for his
life!

Genesis 39:6 describes Joseph as handsome. In
Genesis 29:17, his mother was described the same
way. They are the only two in the Bible who received
such descriptions.

Genesis 39:7–20
Sexual promiscuity was common between slaves.
Joseph was 17 or 18 years old when he entered into
slavery and had been serving Potiphar for 11 years
when this exchange happened. No one would have
known if he compromised. No one back home or
even Potiphar himself. However, Joseph chose to do

what was right even when it would have been easier to cave in.

Joseph refused to sin against:
- the trust given to him
- the woman's husband
- God

How can you relate to Joseph's story?

How does it inspire you to do the right thing even when no one sees or knows?

The contrast between Judah acting the opposite of Joseph is interesting to me. Two boys who were raised in the same home by the same father, yet their views of right and wrong were so different.

Genesis 39:21–23

Prison in Egypt was one of the worst places on earth at that time, yet Joseph's faith never wavered. He knew God would be faithful to what He promised. The chapter ends the same way it began (vv. 2,23). God's blessings are bigger than betrayal, accusations, and position.

How does this give you hope in your own life?

How do you think this chapter would have ended differently if Joseph made different choices?

GENESIS 40

Genesis 40:1
"Some time later" summed up an estimated two years of Joseph's imprisonment: 24 months of waiting; 104 weeks of holding on to what God had promised.
There he sat, thinking of how he had been rejected and falsely accused, yet he never grew bitter.

Genesis 40:4–22
This is leadership: Serving the people God brings into your life.
Joseph helped others with their dreams while trusting God to work on his.

Who are you helping get to their dreams while you are in a waiting season?

Genesis 40:23
Accused, rejected, and now forgotten. You can't read this without your heart breaking for Joseph. Even when men forget about us, God never does!

GENESIS 41

Genesis 41:1–8
Two years passed before Pharaoh dreamed a dream.
Nearly half of Joseph's life up to that point was spent
in either slavery or prison.

Pharaoh searched for an answer that no one could
give. He did not believe in God. At this time in
history, pharaohs actually believed themselves to be
gods. After he searched all the wisdom of men, he was
frustrated and still looked for answers. That is how so
many come to Christ. When we reach the end of our
understanding, we begin our search for what God has.

Note that Joseph initially had two dreams (Genesis
37:5–11) plus the two dreams of the cup bearer and
the baker (Genesis 40:5–19).

Genesis 41:9–14
God has a way of making sure your gifts and talents
come center stage. Suddenly the chief butler
remembered Joseph. In a moment, Joseph's entire life
changed. He received clothing and everything he
needed to go before Pharaoh. When God gets ready
to do something in your life you better be ready!

Read Habakkuk 2:3.

Genesis 41:16,28

His statement seemed small, but standing before someone who did not respect God made this a bold declaration. In all of his years in prison and slavery, Joseph knew his source was God. He knew this was not the time to play it safe or water down what he believed.

Genesis 41:25–37

Joseph's God-given ability to interpret dreams brought him before Pharaoh. His strategy kept him there. Our gift is the God part of who we are. Our strategy is how we develop and prepare ourselves. Joseph didn't waste his time in captivity. He used that time to develop keen leadership skills.

Joseph handed Pharaoh a plan without even knowing he was writing his own job description.

How are you preparing yourself for the opportunities you are believing for?

Genesis 41:38–39

Pharaoh was forced to acknowledge a God that he didn't even believe in. Notice what he praised about Joseph in verse 39.

How would the people in your life describe you?

Genesis 41:40–52

In one day, Joseph went from being a prisoner to second-in-command over all the land. He received a wife and a position of prestige. God knows how to make up for time lost. One day could change your life forever. I am sure there were many days Joseph sat in prison feeling like he was missing out on the life he wanted. In a moment, God gave him every dream in his heart. He had a family, honor, and favor. Three things he did not have for nearly half of his life.

Who bore Joseph's children (v. 50)? What does this say about the relationship he had with Potiphar?

Notice each son's name and their meanings. What is the significance of this?

Remember these two. They are important later.

Genesis 41:53–57
What God said would happen was fulfilled. Their preparation was their choice.

WE CAN KNOW WHAT GOD SAYS WILL HAPPEN AND STILL MAKE THE CHOICE NOT TO PREPARE.

Their preparation made them stand out when the famine occurred.

Little did Joseph know that his preparation would bring his family back into his life.

GENESIS 42

Genesis 42:1
Hard times cause people to come back into your life.
It wasn't their plenty but their lack that brought them
to Joseph.

Genesis 42:4
Imagine how this made the other 10 feel. Leah's
children were optional to Jacob. He loved the
children of Rachel so much more.

Have you ever felt left out or overlooked?

Genesis 42:6
This was the fulfillment of Joseph's dream as a young
boy. (See Genesis 37:5–8.)

Genesis 42:7
This was the only time Joseph showed any hint of
malice. It says that he spoke roughly to them. After all

those years, he didn't lash out or speak out against them for all the hurt they caused.

Genesis 42:8
Joseph wasn't even recognizable. Never would they have thought he would be in the palace.

Genesis 42:13
Their words had to hurt Joseph's heart. To his brothers, he had been dead. How his heart must have ached.

Genesis 42:14–20
Keep in mind, Joseph's mother died at Benjamin's birth. This was his only connection to his mom. I am sure he wondered if Benjamin received the same ill treatment he had.

Why do you think he asked for Benjamin?

Genesis 42:21–22
Guilt has a terrible way of haunting us. Years later, Reuben was still haunted by the day young Joseph was thrown in the pit.

When guilt is our driving force, we accept misfortune as part of our punishment and feel like we must live in the consequences of our mistakes.

What guilt are you holding on to because of something you did in the past?

Genesis 42:23–24
Joseph understood every word, but they were oblivious.

Have you ever overheard a conversation that was hurtful? Or seen an email you shouldn't have seen? If so, you know a portion of the hurt Joseph experienced.

Genesis 42:25–28
When you live in guilt, even blessings seem like a curse. That is why people can experience something good and still feel a sense of dread, because their guilt rejects any good that comes into their life.

Genesis 42:29–38

The brothers returned home and told their father what happened. Notice who spoke up in verse 37.

Jacob made his choice. Keep in mind, Simeon was left behind until they returned with Benjamin. Imagine how this made the sons of Leah feel.

GENESIS 43

Genesis 43:1
Lack caused Jacob to face the decision he had put off.

Genesis 43:11–13
Jacob (Israel) sent more than enough to ensure his sons would be able to bring Benjamin back. He had no idea that the result would be total restoration of what he had lost.

Genesis 43:15–34
They were perplexed at Joseph's request when they arrived. They confessed everything and gave back what wasn't theirs.

They presented Joseph with gifts from their home. Remember they were all young boys when they watched the reunion of their father and uncle (Genesis 33:1–11).

What similarities do you see in their exchange?

How did Jacob's humble approach change the way his sons saw relationships later in life?

Genesis 43:34

Five is the number of grace.

What significance do you think that holds?

GENESIS 44

Genesis 44:1–14

There are a lot of differing opinions on these verses.

Some say Joseph did this so Benjamin would be kept as a slave and Joseph could keep his brother with him.

Others believe Joseph wanted to see if his brothers were still selfish.

Some say it was a mark of favor on Benjamin, similar to the coat of many colors. If that was the case, favor didn't really feel like favor, did it?

Personally, I don't believe Joseph would ever want his brother to be a slave. If he wanted to be cruel, he could have enslaved them all, but we see in his character that he wasn't cruel. Joseph knew his brothers to be selfish, so it didn't need to be tested. I believe Joseph saw a mark of favor on Benjamin and wanted to be certain Benjamin was kept safe. He was fearful of something similar happening to Benjamin that happened to him. Knowing that his brothers acted in foolish ways, he didn't want someone else to pay the price for their poor decisions.

What do you think?

Genesis 44:16
Notice how Judah referred to himself and how his response was similar to Genesis 33:1–11.

Genesis 44:18–34
Judah took a stand. This was the same Judah who slept with a harlot (who was actually his daughter-in-law) then tried to have her killed. Now Judah stood up for what was right to save a life. Many generations later, Jesus was born from Judah's lineage.

What do you think of Judah's boldness?

How have you seen him change throughout our study?

GENESIS 45

Genesis 45:1–8

Joseph revealed his identity and assured his brothers that God was his source.

I have clung to the words of verses 7 and 8 when people have hurt me. I read them out loud, allowing them to sink deep into the wounds of my heart. God has a way of making beauty out of our deepest hurts.

Genesis 45:9–13

True forgiveness looks to the future without any remnant of pain.

Genesis 45:14–15

How can anyone read these verses without tears coming to their eyes?

Can you imagine what his heart felt here?

Genesis 45:17–28

What a beautiful picture of grace and forgiveness. Joseph gave them the best Egypt could offer. When God forgives us, He gives us His best. He doesn't hold any resentment.

Genesis 45:28

God restored to Jacob the one thing he wanted most. It wasn't the gold or silver. It was his son that he cared about.

GENESIS 46

Genesis 46:1
For the first time in a long while, scripture shows Jacob (Israel) making sacrifices. This was a significant place. (See Genesis 21:33, 26:23–25.)

Genesis 46:2–4
God spoke to Israel again, reaffirming what was said before. The sweetness of verse 4 is so special. God let him know that Joseph would be present when he died. I am sure Israel questioned what their relationship would be like. God silenced those fears.

Genesis 46:5–27
What a big caravan of people! Notice how many there are in total (v. 27).

Genesis 46:29
Joseph met his father on the road. He couldn't wait for his arrival! I love this picture of two people reunited after years of separation.

GENESIS 47

Genesis 47:1–6
Joseph used the favor on his life to make sure his family was safe.

Genesis 47:7–12
Joseph gave his family everything they needed. He provided for them in extravagant ways.

Genesis 47:13–26
This was the beginning of the Israelite's slavery. Their lack of preparation for the famine put them in a terrible position. Little by little they sold everything to the Egyptians, not knowing they were enslaving themselves.

The same thing happens today.

OUR LACK OF PREPARATION MAKES US A SLAVE TO THE ENEMY.

Little by little, we forfeit what is ours.

As long as Joseph was in charge, the Israelite people were safe. But the next person in charge wasn't a God-fearing man.

The 20% tax in verse 26 seems high, doesn't it? Most credit cards are 18-24% interest. I don't think that is a coincidence. Most Americans aren't slaves in a physical sense, but they are in a financial sense.

GENESIS 48

Genesis 48:1–11

On his death bed, Israel reflected on these things:

- The blessing of God at Bethel. Do you remember the significance of that moment? He had left his mother and was fleeing from his brother. On his death bed, he still remembered the covenant God made with him there.

- He remembered Rachel. No mention of Leah. He recalled the day of her death as his approached. The love he had for her is the sweetest of all the stories in the Bible. He never stopped loving her.

- His thankfulness for restoration with Joseph. Time had not worn off his gratitude for his son.

Genesis 48:12–20

This significant portion of Scripture is symbolic of the gentile church receiving the blessing of God and being made heirs according the covenant of Abraham.

This moment is so important that the writer of Hebrews recalls it in Hebrews 11:21.

GENESIS 49

Genesis 47–49 are Jacob's (Israel's) deathbed scenes. These were his final moments where he laid out the inheritance of his 12 sons. The words spoken weren't by chance. They were prophetic unctions from God that were carried out for generations to come. Although Jacob played favorites all his life, in his final moments *all* of his sons were called to his bedside for a blessing.

From these men, the 12 tribes of Israel mentioned throughout the Bible were formed. (See James 1:1.) Here is a map of their settlements.

Let's look at each of the 12 and their blessings.

Reuben and Gad
Genesis 49:3–4, 19
Remember that Reuben lost his inheritance because of his disobedience (Genesis 35:22). Neither Reuben nor Gad received a full blessing from Jacob. The Bible tells what later became of their line. Reuben and Gad's descendants made the choice not to go into the Promised Land with the Israelite people. (See Numbers 32:4–7 and Joshua 1:11–15.) After that, the tribes of Reuben and Gad fall off the pages of the Bible. We do not hear much of them again.

What reasons do they give for not entering the Promised Land in Numbers 32:4?

Do you think it is the same complacency that Reuben initially had in Genesis 35:22 that is seen generations later in Numbers 32:4?

How have you allowed complacency to talk you out of what God has for you?

Simeon and Levi
Genesis 49:5–7
Remember these were the brothers who came to Dinah's defense and defeated Shechem's city in Genesis 34. Later in history when the Israelite people made a golden calf, the Levites stood with Moses. (See Exodus 32:25.) The Levites became a tribe of priests and consequently weren't allowed to own land. Simeon resided near Judah but later dispersed around Israel.

Judah
Genesis 49:8–12
Judah made his fair share of mistakes. However, Jacob (Israel) under the influence of the Holy Spirit made a declaration over him that wouldn't be fully realized until Jesus. Judah, as a tribe, is mentioned more throughout the Bible than the other 12. King Solomon, David, Mary, and Jesus all came from this tribe. Jesus was referred to as the Lion of the Tribe of Judah, first prophetically by Jacob in this blessing (v. 9) and later in Revelation 5:5.

Judah's portion of land later became Jerusalem. Verse 11 is echoed in Isaiah 63:1–3 as the prophet Isaiah foretold that their Redeemer (Jesus) would come. Jesus fulfills this prophecy in Revelation 19:11–16.

Zebulun
Genesis 49:13
This tribe made up a significant portion of David's army. (See 1 Chronicles 12:33.) They were a tribe of strong people who were loyal to the Kings and Judges they served.

Issachar
Genesis 49:14–15
Not much is known about the tribe of Issachar. They were wise men who gave counsel to the government of Israel (1 Chronicles 12:32).

Dan
Genesis 49:16–18
Sadly, the tribe of Dan did not follow God's plan for their lives. They were mentioned often in scripture as defying God's people. They didn't go into the Promised Land. They surrendered their inheritance and turned to idol worship. Samson was a descendant of the tribe of Dan. Some call Dan the "lost" tribe of Israel. Not much is said of the tribe of Dan after 722 BC. Even when the tribes are mentioned in Revelation, Dan is not.

Nephtali
Genesis 49:21
One small verse was given to this son. However, a significant prophecy was given about him in Isaiah 9 that said the Messiah would dwell in their land. Their land was Galilee where Jesus spent much of His ministry.

Joseph
Genesis 49:22–26
Joseph's land was divided to his two sons, Manasseh and Ephraim. Even though his land was divided, he received a double inheritance of everything. Although Ephraim was younger, he received the blessing of the first born. From his lineage came the prophet Samuel (the one who anointed Saul and David to be king) and Joshua (who led the Israelites into the Promised Land). When the Israelites came into the Promised Land, the Bible mentions the descendants of

Manasseh and Ephraim as the only tribes out of the 12 who dwelt on both sides of the Jordan.

Benjamin
Genesis 49:27
The blessing he received from his father, Jacob, was not encouraging. I am sure the brothers were shocked at the words their father spoke. However, both King Saul and Paul the Apostle came from the tribe of Benjamin. Though the tribe was small in land mass, they later held their ground in Judges 20 and 21.

Genesis 49:29–33
Jacob drew up his feet and breathed his last breath. His body was taken to Hebron, the land Abraham had purchased from the Hittites (Genesis 23). At his request, Jacob's body was placed with Abraham, Sarah, Isaac, Rebekah, and his wife Leah. Although I personally think he wished to be with his beloved Rachel above all else.

GENESIS 50

Genesis 50:1–14

Jacob passed away. He was a giant among the patriarchs of the Old Testament. He was often hard to love, but we see much of ourselves in Jacob. The words of verse 3 pierce my heart, "the Egyptians wept and grieved for him [in public mourning as they would for royalty] for seventy days."

What honor Joseph gave his father. For the short amount of time they were reunited, he ensured that his father was held in high regard among the people. What a beautiful testimony of the heart of Joseph.

Genesis 50:12–21

Sweet Joseph always did what was right and kind. The brothers feared that with their father's death, their good fortune would end. Joseph modeled what true forgiveness looks like. His focus remained on God only. He reminded his brothers that God worked everything together for his good. I often wonder if this scene played through Paul's mind when he wrote Romans 8:28.

Genesis 50:22–26

I wonder why the author of Genesis left out so much of the rest of Joseph's life. It doesn't tell of a large procession or grand funeral. There was no scandal in his final moments like that of Jacob and Esau. No final remarks or blessings on his sons. Scripture simply tells that he lived a long full life. He saw his grandchildren and great grandchildren. His only recorded words were to his brothers that God would be with them as He was with Abraham, Isaac, and Jacob. Oh those words couldn't be more true. Joseph knew because he had seen it fulfilled in his lifetime.

So the story of Genesis ends. What began with a love story of God sharing creation with His people, was marked with failures, betrayal, hatred, and the like, then ends with love, forgiveness, and God's redemption. There is truly no book in the Bible as beautiful as Genesis. In it is found the foundation for the rest of all scripture. In its pages, we find God's original desire for all mankind: relationship. This is just beginning of all that is to come, and the story continues.

ABOUT CRYSTAL SPARKS

Crystal Sparks is a writer, speaker, and pastor who is passionate about encouraging people to fulfill the dreams that God has placed in their heart. Raised in the small Texas town of Sulphur Springs, Crystal's life was profoundly transformed when she encountered God in the midst of her difficult teenage years.

In her 16 years of ministry, she has served in the role of Youth Pastor, Associate Pastor, and Lead Pastor. Crystal has spoken for various sports teams, youth events, church conferences, and women's gatherings both nationally and internationally. In 2014, she relocated with her husband Bryan and their two children, Brailey and Bear, to plant a life-giving church. Together, Crystal and Bryan serve as Lead Pastors of One Church.

www.crystalsparks.org

GET A FREE BOOK ABOUT UNDERSTANDING SCRIPTURE

Building a relationship with my readers is the very best thing about what I do. I occasionally send out devotionals, special offers, new releases and information about upcoming events.

If you sign up for my mailing list I'll send you a copy of my book, Understanding Scripture. This book helps break down and demystify reading your Bible.

You can get the book for free by signing up at www.crystalsparks.org/genesis

Talk soon!

Crystal Sparks

Enjoy this book? You can make a big difference!

Every review and share on social media helps so much to get the word out! I am always amazed at how one review or one person talking about it to a friend gets the book passed to the next person. I truly have the most committed and loyal bunch of readers.